ANYTHINK LIBRARIES/
RANGEVIEW LIBRARY DISTRICT

D0475118

Humanity's greatest advances are
not in its discoveries—but in how
those discoveries are applied to
reduce inequity.

—BILL GATES

Think Smart
Be Fearless

A Biography of **BILL GATES**

Sharon Mentyka   Illustrated by **Vivien Mildenberger**

little bigfoot

an imprint of sasquatch books
seattle, wa

Many years ago, in a sparkling blue-green city by the sea, a bouncing baby boy was born three days before Halloween.

There was never a doubt what his name would be. William Henry Gates—the third in his family to be given his great-grandfather's name.

But William Henry Gates III was an awfully big name for such a little baby.

Then Gami, who loved all games, remembered the cardplayer's word for "three."

"Trey!" she announced. That sorted it out.

LET'S CALL HIM TREY!

Trey was a curious boy right from the start.

His parents taught him to work hard, give back, and speak up for what he believed in. Growing up, Trey learned that if he had a question, the answer existed somewhere. All he had to do was find it.

He also played games, lots of them. In Trey's family, games were as intense as work and just as competitive.

Gami taught him double solitaire, fish, gin, and bridge—even a little poker.

Trey knew the games were all in fun. But he also knew how good it felt when his name was called as the winner.

As Seattle prepared to host the 1962 World's Fair, six-year-old Trey watched, enchanted, as the city's new Space Needle climbed up-up-up. It seemed to be pointing toward a limitless future.

At the fair, Trey rode the one-mile monorail again and again. He visited every pavilion, exploring exhibits of satellites, NASA's *Friendship 7* capsule, and a computer the size of a small room!

Trey's imagination soared too. Now he didn't just want to learn about *some* things. He wanted to learn about *everything*.

He decided to always think smart.

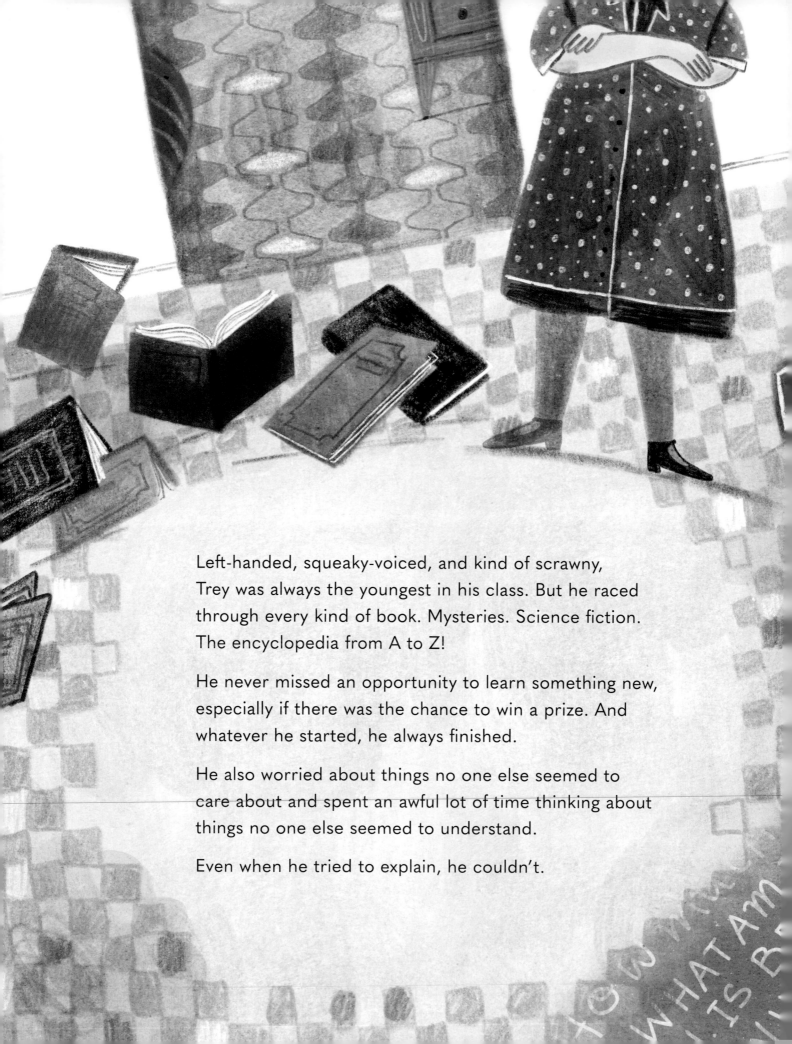

Left-handed, squeaky-voiced, and kind of scrawny,
Trey was always the youngest in his class. But he raced
through every kind of book. Mysteries. Science fiction.
The encyclopedia from A to Z!

He never missed an opportunity to learn something new,
especially if there was the chance to win a prize. And
whatever he started, he always finished.

He also worried about things no one else seemed to
care about and spent an awful lot of time thinking about
things no one else seemed to understand.

Even when he tried to explain, he couldn't.

Trey liked doing everything fast. But sometimes his fast thinking didn't always work out.

So he found other things to be curious about and started to pick and choose where to earn his As (reading and math, of course). Looking back, it all made sense. But at the time it felt like trouble.

His parents began to worry. Maybe something had to change.

And so, despite their devotion to public education, they made a decision, hoping Seattle's most respected private school would help Trey to thrive.

At Lakeside, "Trey" became "Bill."

His new school had lots of unusual rules. Teachers needed to be called "masters." The dress code called for button-down shirts and long pants. Everyone had assigned places for lunch. And there were no girls allowed.

It took Bill a while to adjust, until slowly he stumbled into the math-and-science crowd, led by a cool older boy named Paul Allen.

Could it be that Bill had finally found a place to fit in or, at least, not stick out quite so much? Soon they are inseparable—a band of headstrong, spirited boys on a mission.

One day something remarkable happened. In a tiny stuffy room, Bill and his friends discovered something amazing. Who would have thought the school's Mothers' Club could purchase something so fabulous by selling old clothing at a rummage sale?

The ASR-33 Teletype was big and clunky, with paper tape that jammed, but it could connect over the phone lines to the big mainframe computers miles away. To Bill, it represented the future.

Suddenly everything clicked.

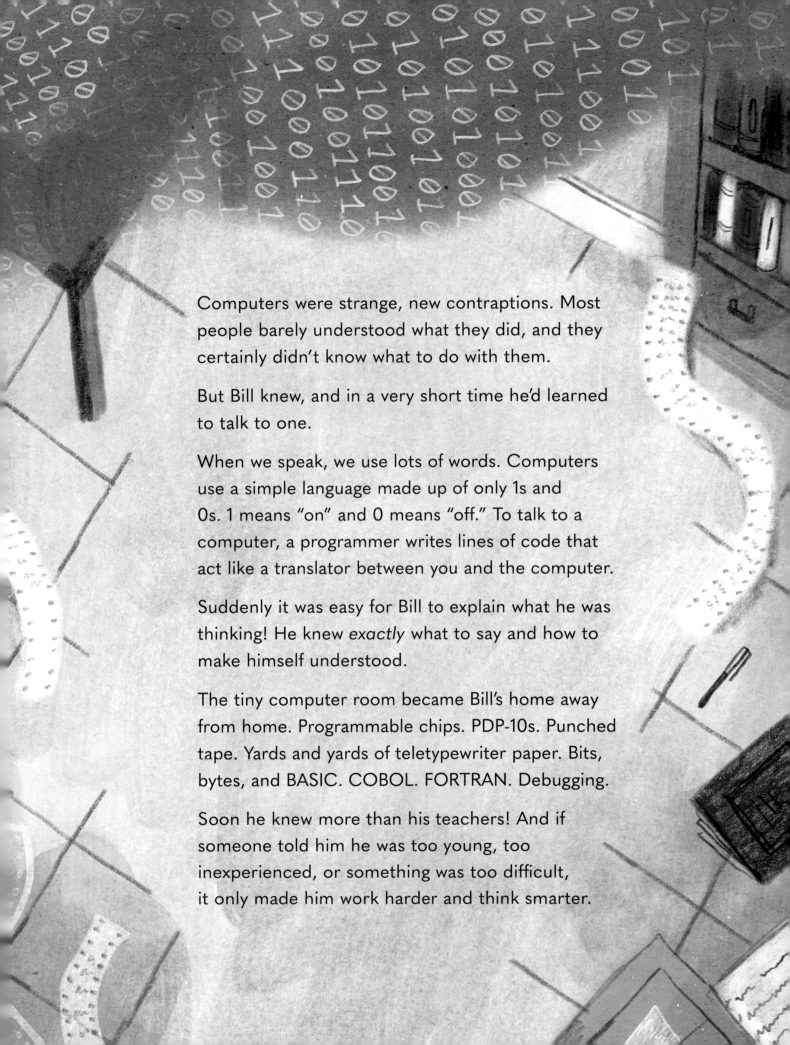

Computers were strange, new contraptions. Most people barely understood what they did, and they certainly didn't know what to do with them.

But Bill knew, and in a very short time he'd learned to talk to one.

When we speak, we use lots of words. Computers use a simple language made up of only 1s and 0s. 1 means "on" and 0 means "off." To talk to a computer, a programmer writes lines of code that act like a translator between you and the computer.

Suddenly it was easy for Bill to explain what he was thinking! He knew *exactly* what to say and how to make himself understood.

The tiny computer room became Bill's home away from home. Programmable chips. PDP-10s. Punched tape. Yards and yards of teletypewriter paper. Bits, bytes, and BASIC. COBOL. FORTRAN. Debugging.

Soon he knew more than his teachers! And if someone told him he was too young, too inexperienced, or something was too difficult, it only made him work harder and think smarter.

He couldn't explain it, but Bill had a sneaking suspicion that someday people would use computers in a way that would change the world.

Bill knew he wanted to be part of that change.

The next stop was college. Three letters of acceptance arrived. Bill made his choice.

One snowy December day in 1974 in Cambridge, Massachusetts, Paul burst into Bill's dorm room at Harvard with exciting news!

A company in New Mexico had just developed a personal computer kit for hobbyists—the Altair 8800. As soon as Bill read the article, he knew this was the chance he'd been waiting for!

On its own a computer isn't very smart. It's just a machine made with wires and switches. If computers were going to be in every home, Bill knew they would need software to really work—lines of code telling the computer to turn those switches "on" or "off."

Bill and Paul jumped at the challenge. There was no way they were going to let the home computer revolution arrive without them.

So Bill disguised his squeaky voice, called the makers of the Altair 8800, and finagled a meeting to share their new software.

Except it wasn't true—they hadn't written any code at all! Even worse, neither Bill nor Paul knew exactly *how* to write it. Without a real Altair computer to work with, they'd be doing a lot of guessing.

But it didn't matter. Bill wasn't afraid. He knew the answer was out there somewhere. He just needed to find it.

Bill and Paul worked night and day making new and complicated changes to the BASIC computer programming language so it could be used on the Altair 8800.

Bill wrote and rewrote thousands of lines of code, making them short . . . shorter . . . the shortest they could be.

In computer code, short lines are important.

Finally, eight weeks later, they were ready.

While Bill waited and worried in Cambridge, Paul traveled to New Mexico to demonstrate their new software. Would it work?

Two thousand miles away, Paul loaded the program into the Altair on a paper tape. The machine flashed "READY." He typed "PRINT 2 + 2," hit "Return," and waited.

Immediately, the Altair clickety-clacked back its answer: "4." This had never been done before.

Bill and Paul had just made history.

A new company, Microsoft, was born.

Bill decided to quit school, promising his parents he'd finish one day, and joined Paul in New Mexico.

He had a lot to learn, but little by little he proved he could deliver what he promised. (Usually he promised first and figured it out later. But that was okay. Bill knew he would always finish what he started.)

At first Bill was too young to even rent a car to go to meetings. His secretary made sure his hair was combed. She checked that his suits weren't too rumpled. And she worried.

But soon Bill began to miss the trees, the water, and the mountains of the Pacific Northwest. He decided to go home.

ORIGINAL MICROSOFT EMPLOYEES

Little by little, Microsoft grew. So did the pressure and responsibilities.

A job with Bill meant unlimited soda, coding challenges, the freedom to experiment, and generous stock options. It also meant round-the-clock work, impossible deadlines, and, sometimes, angry rants and rages from a nervous boss.

Bill had become used to computers doing *exactly* what he told them to do. Now he expected the same from his employees. He knew everyone's license plate. He would scan the parking lot, keeping track of who came in late and left early. People learned to sleep standing up.

Bill worked hard too, reviewing every line of code written, worrying about every tiny detail, never taking one day off in ten years.

He worried so much that he forgot to eat. He worried so much he forgot to sleep. He worried so much he forgot what it was he should be worrying about.

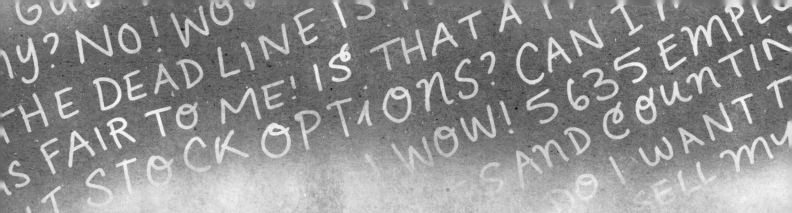

Soon Microsoft had deals in Japan and Europe with IBM and Apple. Bigwigs came calling, wanting to buy his company. Bill sent them a nice "No" letter and continued on as Chief Worrier.

Many years passed. Thirty-year-old Bill still looked like a nineteen-year-old, but it didn't matter anymore. Once he entered a room, it was crystal clear who was the boss. Thousands of people all over the world worked for him now. That's a lot of brains doing a lot of thinking!

Bill's dream had become real. His software had changed the way ordinary people worked and played. Computers were popping up in offices and homes everywhere!

But sometimes Bill felt lonely. Microsoft kept getting bigger and bigger. Bill's job kept getting harder and harder. The whole world was watching, wondering what he would promise next.

This was *not* how he'd planned it. Maybe it was time for things to change.

Melinda arrived at the perfect moment. They loved all the same things—dancing, Willie Nelson, and *The Sound of Music*. And he could make her laugh!

It would take Bill many more years to puzzle out what his next big challenges would be. When he did, he'd have Melinda and his mother to thank.

From those to whom much is given, much is expected.

Mom

People wrote to Bill all the time asking for money. Sometimes the requests were sad: money for food or to help pay hospital bills. Sometimes they just seemed silly!

Bill and his father read almost all the letters and thought long and hard about how they could help. Finally Bill decided to use some of his millions to start a foundation—an organization whose main purpose would be to begin the process of giving back that his mother taught him.

Now it was time to read, think, and study again.

Every life has equal value. If you had a few hours and a few dollars to give to help improve people's lives, where would you spend your time and money?

If Bill was going to give money away, he wanted to think smart about where it would do the most good.

India

Africa

One day Bill and Melinda read an article that shocked them.

Millions of children in poor countries around the world were dying every year from diseases Bill thought could be prevented. Measles, malaria, polio, yellow fever, even diarrhea.

How could this be? Vaccines for these diseases could save lives, and they cost less than a dollar! Didn't anyone care?

Bill decided to turn caring into action.

Sure, working to eliminate childhood infectious diseases was complicated, but complexity had never stopped Bill. The first half of his life had been good preparation for the second half.

Some people thought he was being arrogant. Bill saw his ideas as fearless thinking. Why set limits on what you think you can achieve?

Bill began spending less and less time at his day job and more and more time thinking about how his foundation could make a difference in people's lives.

Now he travels around the world, checking facts, understanding the problems, analyzing what's needed, and calculating what it will all cost.

People ask him all the time what he wants to be remembered for. Legacy is a stupid thing, he tells them. (Bill thinks *lots* of ideas are stupid.)

Bill has received many honors for his life's work—the National Medal of Technology and Innovation, the Global Humanitarian Award, and the Presidential Medal of Freedom. He's even been knighted by Queen Elizabeth II of England! But an honorary Doctor of Laws degree from Harvard makes him happiest—now he's kept the promise he made to his parents to finish college!

When Bill announces plans to give away 95 percent of his money in his lifetime, he also challenges others who are wealthy to do the same.

Many do, pledging to follow Bill's lead, stepping up to the plate of fearless thinking.

More about
Bill Gates

Curiosity to Last a Lifetime

The extraordinary life and accomplishments of Bill Gates were shaped right from the start by his extraordinary parents. Bill was born on October 28, 1955, in Seattle, Washington, and his family's Northwest roots can be traced back to the 1800s.

His father, William H. Gates Sr., a shy, six-foot-seven lawyer and civil activist, is a kind, generous man who set high expectations for his children. Show up for life, he would write one day. Use your gifts and have no regrets. His mother, Mary Maxwell Gates, spent her life reaching out and connecting people and served on the boards of major corporations and nonprofits. Bill recalls many times tagging along with her to meetings. Along with inheriting her smile, Bill learned from Mary that one person can truly make a difference in someone's world.

Bill and his siblings, Kristi and Libby, were encouraged to take risks in this safe, supportive environment. Bill learned that if he failed at something—which he did many times—he could always try again, and next time he might have better success.

The Right School at the Right Time

The decision to send Bill to Lakeside School was critical to his later success. Lakeside not only introduced Bill to computers, but it was there where he met Paul Allen, the man with whom he would later cofound Microsoft. The school provided fertile ground for Bill to play, explore, and experiment—essentially providing a hands-on apprenticeship in what we now call STEM (science, technology, engineering, and math). He even wrote a computer program for the school to manage students' class schedules—a difficult task even for someone of his ability—and cleverly arranged his own schedule with no classes on Fridays. Lakeside gave Bill what he later described as the three key components of a great education—rigor, relevance, and relationships.

A Computer in Every Home

When Bill was born, fewer than 500 computers existed in the entire world. Personal computers were virtually unknown and the term *software* had not yet made it into everyday vocabulary.

Computers were huge mainframes that cost millions of dollars. Businesses and schools paid a fee to connect with them over phone lines using a teletype machine like the one Bill used at Lakeside. Originally designed for Western Union, the Teletype ASR (Automatic Send and Receive) was almost totally a mechanical machine. It consisted of a keyboard and tape reader for input, a printer for display, and a paper tape reader and punch for input/output. The only electronic part was the power supply. Later models included a built-in telephone modem to connect to a mainframe computer.

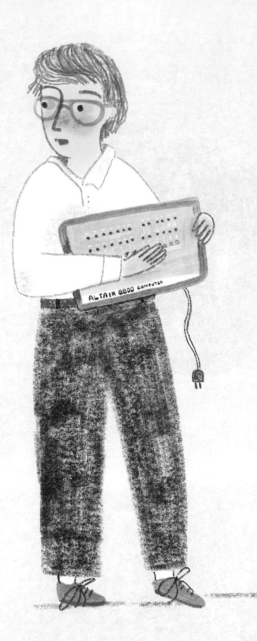

Teletypes were the perfect all-in-one devices for early microcomputer users and hobbyists, offering the only reliable way to store and retrieve programs. In the late 1960s and '70s, you could see and hear them clacking away in the background of the evening news as part of the AP Wire Service.

Back then being a math-and-science kid wasn't cool like it is today. The 1960s were turbulent times. Many students focused their energy on protest marches and anti-war demonstrations. But the STEM field was beginning to take root in small ways.

By the time Bill started college, microchips had begun to replace transistors in computers, greatly reducing a computer's physical size. The Altair 8800 was the first "hobby" computer, and it was sold in a kit for about $400. The Altair had no keyboard, no screen, 4KB of memory (today's smartphones have about four million times that amount!), and most importantly, no software to tell the computer what to do, draw, or count. Without software written by computer programmers, a computer is basically just a metal box.

Bill called his decision to write software for the Altair "the most important idea I ever had," because it ushered in the era of the personal computer. He accurately predicted that someday there would be "a computer in every home" and people would be able to look up any information they needed when they needed it.

It must not have been easy for Bill's family, who valued education almost above all else, when he decided to quit Harvard to start Micro-Soft (the name was a combination of "micro" for *microcomputer* and "soft" for *software*). But true to their nature, his parents gave him the support and freedom to meet life on his own terms.

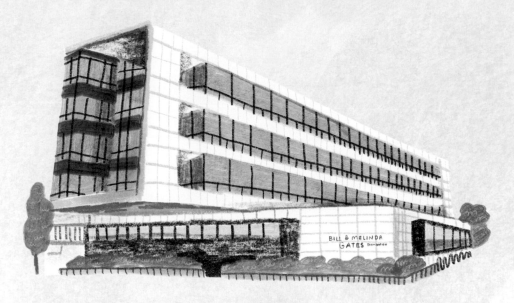

Impatient Optimists

Meeting his future wife, Melinda, and starting a family had a huge impact on shifting Bill's focus beyond his work at Microsoft. Bill had spent years building up a billion-dollar company. As a scientist he became very good at asking self-critical questions that mattered. He realized that no one person could possibly use all the money he had in one lifetime. He wanted his children to find what he did—their own work that they are passionate about.

And so after his mother died, with Melinda's support, he began to think seriously about moving his focus from business to philanthropy—the process of giving back.

The work that Bill is undertaking through the Bill & Melinda Gates Foundation may be even greater than his innovations at Microsoft. With assets over $50 billion, it is the single largest private philanthropic foundation in the world, working to improve global health, education, and clean energy.

Bill and Melinda have set ambitious goals—to eradicate polio, malaria, and other childhood diseases; to eliminate hunger and extreme poverty; and to improve the lives of ordinary people from Seattle to South Africa. The task is daunting, but Bill believes in the power and rippling effect of individual commitments and choices. He calls himself an "impatient optimist."

He knows it takes more than money to make these dreams come true. It takes vision, commitment, and focus. And he knows he can't do it alone. It's going to take a lot of people working together. Just imagine the innovation and ideas young people today could bring to life if they have the opportunity to develop STEM skills! Let's all join Bill by thinking smart and being fearless.

Timeline

~1837

Mathematician Charles Babbage designs the Analytical Engine, a machine with all the essential parts of a modern computer.

1843

Mathematician Ada Lovelace publishes what is now considered the first computer program, instructions for calculating numbers on Babbage's machine.

1936

Mathematician Alan Turing develops the basic principle of modern computing—controlling its operations with automatic coded instructions in the computer's memory.

1962

The first computer game, *Spacewar!*, runs on a computer the size of a large car at Massachusetts Institute of Technology (MIT).

1963

The ASR-33 Teletype, made for Western Union, becomes a popular input/output device for the first generation of microcomputers.

1964

IBM introduces the first word processor, the Magnetic Tape Selectric Typewriter.

Thomas Kurtz and John Kemeny create BASIC (Beginner's All-Purpose Symbolic Instruction Code), an easy-to-learn programming language.

1971

Intel introduces the first microprocessor chip, the Intel 4004.

1973–74

Bill enrolls as a pre-law student at Harvard University.

Ed Roberts of Micro Instrumentation and Telemetry Systems (MITS) designs the Altair 8800, a small personal computer kit for hobbyists, and markets it in *Popular Electronics*.

1975

Bill writes and sells BASIC software for the Altair 8800 to MITS; he takes a leave of absence from Harvard and cofounds Micro-Soft with Paul Allen in Albuquerque, New Mexico.

1980

Microsoft signs a contract with IBM, the world's largest mainframe computer company, to write the operating-system software for their new personal computers.

1981

IBM introduces the IBM PC, with 16KB of memory, running MS-DOS.

1985

Microsoft introduces the Windows operating system, allowing users to interact with their computer using a mouse rather than by typing commands on the keyboard.

Bill Gates' life and the evolution of the computer industry are closely intertwined. In the following timeline, significant events in the history of computers are noted with gray dots and dates. Milestones and personal accomplishments in Bill's life are highlighted in red. Overlapping dates contain both colored dots.

1951

Remington Rand introduces the first commercial computer in the United States—the UNIVAC (UNIVersal Automatic Computer), as big as a room and able to store one thousand words in its memory.

1952

Mathematician Grace Hopper completes A-0, a program that uses written words instead of numbers to give instructions to the computer.

1955

Bill Gates is born in Seattle, Washington, on October 28.

1966

Star Trek, the popular television series, debuts with its imagined computer technologies such as voice recognition, handheld computing, and human-computer interaction.

1967

Bill enrolls in Lakeside School, Seattle, Washington.

1968

Bill writes his first computer program, a tic-tac-toe game in BASIC, on the ASR-33 Teletype.

Oregon inventor Douglas Engelbart unveils the first computer mouse.

1976

Company is renamed Microsoft; Bill raises the issue of software piracy in his "Open Letter to Hobbyists."

Apple Computers is founded by Steve Wozniak and Steve Jobs.

1978

The first computers are installed in the White House.

1979

Bill moves Microsoft's headquarters to Bellevue, Washington.

1986–87

Bill becomes the youngest billionaire at age thirty-one after Microsoft becomes a publicly traded company.

1988

Over forty-five million PCs are in use across the United States.

1990

The World Wide Web is born.

1994

Bill marries Melinda French in Hawaii; Bill's mother Mary dies; Bill establishes the William H. Gates Foundation with an endowment of $106 million.

1997

IBM's computer Deep Blue wins its first chess game against world champion Garry Kasparov.

2000

Bill resigns as CEO of Microsoft and establishes the Bill & Melinda Gates Foundation.

2008

Bill leaves his day job at Microsoft.

2010

Bill establishes the Giving Pledge with Warren Buffett to inspire "billionaires or those who would be if not for their giving" to designate the majority of their wealth to philanthropy.

2011

IBM's supercomputer Watson—a "question-answering" machine that uses artificial intelligence (AI)—defeats two *Jeopardy!* champions.

Glossary

Bit: A unit of computer information, either "1" or "0," that a computer reads as "on" or "off" or "yes" or "no"

Byte: A group of eight bits that work together as a unit in computer memory

Code: A set of instructions telling a computer what to do

Computer: An electronic device that stores and processes information

Computer language: A system of written symbols and rules that "talk" to a computer, such as BASIC, COBOL, and FORTRAN

Debugging: The process of finding and fixing errors that prevent a computer from working correctly—a term popularized by mathematician Grace Hopper who discovered a moth had shorted out the Mark II computer at Harvard

Electronics: Devices and circuits designed using transistors and microchips

Entrepreneur: Someone who proposes a new idea or business and often takes on financial risks

Foundation: An organization that dedicates a sizable amount of money to be used for research or charity

Hardware: The physical machine and wiring of a computer or other electronic device

Humanitarian: A person or idea that seeks to better the lives of people

Innovation: A method, idea, or product that solves a problem in a new way

2005

Bill receives honorary knighthood from Queen Elizabeth II of England.

2006

The verb *google* is added to the dictionary, prompted by the Google search engine.

2007

Bill receives honorary Doctor of Laws degree from Harvard University.

2017

To date the Bill & Melinda Gates Foundation has given away $45.5 billion in grants to fight hunger, disease, and poverty.

Mainframe: A large high-speed computer that supports multiple smaller systems

Malaria: A disease transmitted by mosquitoes in many tropical regions of the world

Microcomputer: A small personal computer that uses a microchip to run its systems

Operating system: Software that controls how a computer does its work

Philanthropist: Someone who works to help others through the donation of money to good causes

Polio: An infectious disease of the nervous system, especially in young children, that can cause muscle weakness and paralysis

Programmer: Someone who writes instructions in a language that a computer can understand

Punched tape: Paper tape punched with holes that communicate information to a computer

Software: The operating information and programs that tell a computer what to do

Stock options: A benefit that allows employees of a company to own a share of the company

Technology: The branch of science applied to practical purposes in society or business

Teletypewriter: A machine that prints messages sent over a telephone line

Trey: A number three playing card or a die with three spots

For Lena, another fearless Lakeside grad.—SM

To Mat. Together we are fearless.—VM

Copyright © 2019 by Sharon Mentyka
Illustrations copyright © 2019 by Vivien Mildenberger

All rights reserved. No portion of this book may be reproduced or utilized in any form, or by any electronic, mechanical, or other means, without the prior written permission of the publisher.

Manufactured in China by C&C Offset Printing Co. Ltd. Shenzhen, Guangdong Province, in May 2019

LITTLE BIGFOOT with colophon is a registered trademark of Penguin Random House LLC

23 22 21 20 19   9 8 7 6 5 4 3 2 1

Editors: Christy Cox, Ben Clanton
Production editor: Bridget Sweet
Design: Tony Ong

Quote on front endsheet from the *Harvard Gazette*
Photo on page 40 by Bruce Burgess

Library of Congress Cataloging-in-Publication Data
Names: Mentyka, Sharon, author. | Mildenberger, Vivien, illustrator.
Title: Think smart, be fearless : a biography of Bill Gates / Sharon Mentyka
   ; illustrated by Vivien Mildenberger.
Description: Seattle : Little Bigfoot, [2019] | Audience: Age 5-9. |
   Audience: Grade K to 3.
Identifiers: LCCN 2019003938 | ISBN 9781632171764 (hardcover)
Subjects: LCSH: Gates, Bill, 1955---Juvenile literature. |
   Businesspeople--United States--Biography--Juvenile literature. | Computer
   software industry--United States--Juvenile literature.
Classification: LCC HD9696.2.U62 G376 2019 | DDC 338.7/61004092 [B] --dc23
LC record available at https://lccn.loc.gov/2019003938

ISBN: 978-1-63217-176-4

Sasquatch Books
1904 Third Avenue, Suite 710
Seattle, WA 98101
SasquatchBooks.com

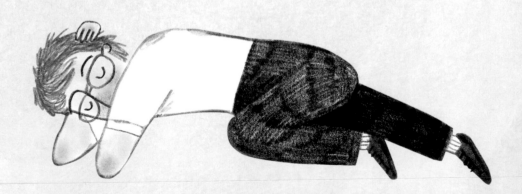